FOOTBALL

Toughness on the Gridiron

PREPARING FOR GAME DAY

BASEBALL & SOFTBALL: SUCCESS ON THE DIAMOND

BASKETBALL: STRATEGY ON THE HARDWOOD

CHEERLEADING: TECHNIQUES FOR PERFORMING

EXTREME SPORTS: POINTERS FOR PUSHING THE LIMITS

FOOTBALL: TOUGHNESS ON THE GRIDIRON

LACROSSE: FACING OFF ON THE FIELD

SOCCER: BREAKING AWAY ON THE PITCH

TRACK & FIELD: CONDITIONING FOR GREATNESS

VOLLEYBALL: APPROACHING THE NET

WRESTLING: CONTENDING ON THE MAT

PREPARING FOR GAME DAY

FOOTBALL
Toughness on the Gridiron

Peter Douglas

MASON CREST

Mason Crest
450 Parkway Drive, Suite D
Broomall, Pennsylvania 19008
(866) MCP-BOOK (toll free)

First printing
9 8 7 6 5 4 3 2 1

ISBN (hardback) 978-1-4222-3917-9
ISBN (series) 978-1-4222-3912-4
ISBN (ebook) 978-1-4222-7872-7

Cataloging-in-Publication Data on file with the Library of Congress

QR CODES AND LINKS TO THIRD-PARTY CONTENT

CONTENTS

KEY ICONS TO LOOK FOR:

Words to understand: These words with their easy-to-understand definitions will increase the reader's understanding of the text while building vocabulary skills.

Sidebars: This boxed material within the main text allows readers to build knowledge, gain insights, explore possibilities, and broaden their perspectives by weaving together additional information to provide realistic and holistic perspectives.

Educational Videos: Readers can view videos by scanning our QR codes, providing them with additional educational content to supplement the text. Examples include news coverage, moments in history, speeches, iconic sports moments and much more!

Text-dependent questions: These questions send the reader back to the text for more careful attention to the evidence presented there.

Research projects: Readers are pointed toward areas of further inquiry connected to each chapter. Suggestions are provided for projects that encourage deeper research and analysis.

Series glossary of key terms: This back-of-the book glossary contains terminology used throughout this series. Words found here increase the reader's ability to read and comprehend higher-level books and articles in this field.

 ### WORDS TO UNDERSTAND:

conversely: in a contrary or opposite way, on the other hand

gluteus maximus: the broad, thick, outermost muscle of the buttocks, involved in the rotation and extension of the thigh

ordained: ordered or commanded

Chapter 1

GAME DAY

Football game days are a ritual across America. On Fridays during football season, people flock to watch their local high school teams play under the lights. On Saturdays, the focus shifts to the college game as major schools get national attention for matchups with conference rivals. And then of course there is Sunday, when the National Football League (NFL) dominates the sporting landscape and, to a large degree, the cultural landscape as well.

Just as fans have their Friday, Saturday, and Sunday rituals, the players who entertain them have rituals of their own, which they perform faithfully to help themselves to be ready to play on game day. These rituals include both the physical and the mental aspects of preparation.

> "Football is like life—it requires perseverance, self-denial, hard work, sacrifice, dedication and respect for authority."
>
> – NFL and Super Bowl champion coach Vince Lombardi, Jr.

> *To me, football is so much about mental toughness, it's digging deep, it's doing whatever you need to do to help a team win and that comes in a lot of shapes and forms.*

Two-time NFL MVP QB Tom Brady

REST

In terms of preparation, game day starts by getting the proper amount of rest. It is recommended that people on average need seven to eight hours of sleep each night. Athletes need more rest than most people as they push their bodies in games and practices and therefore need more time to recover.

Doctors say sleep has a big impact on what happens to your body. The body uses sleep as a time to repair itself, and when athletes do not get enough sleep, they lose out on this valuable time, which they need much more than the average person. Studies have shown that more is better when it comes to sleep. A study of the Stanford University basketball team, for example, tracked the sleep of players for several months. Over the course of the study, players added an average of almost two hours of sleep a night to their normal amount. The results were clear. Players improved their performance, i.e. increasing their speed by 5 percent. They also increased free throw percentages by 9 percent. Testing showed that they had faster reflexes, and they reported feeling happier.

Some people have more trouble going to and staying asleep than others. Here are some tips to help get a good night's sleep before a game:

- Cut out caffeine and alcohol. Both substances have adverse affects on the ability to sleep well.

- Cut out sleep meds. Other than something specific prescribed by a doctor, sleep aid pills are more likely to hinder sleep quality than improve it.

- Get on a regular schedule, waking up and going to sleep at the same times.

- If you have to travel and the schedule gets disrupted, try to maintain as close to a normal schedule as possible.

Professional and college players also commonly supplement their sleep with game day naps, ranging in length from thirty minutes to three hours.

"On the fade route, the first thing you want to remember, you gotta keep your shoulders low and your hands up, because the first thing the DB's going to try to do is get his hands on your chest to slow you down."

– Six-time Pro Bowl WR Calvin Johnson

EAT

Football players need plenty of food to fuel their efforts. They tend to be bigger on average than most athletes and therefore need to get a lot of calories before games.

Experts suggest a balance of carbohydrates, protein, and fruits and vegetables at a ratio of 2:1:1, respectively. The pregame meal should be eaten about four hours before the game. Also, about an hour before kickoff, players can go for a carb boost with an energy-rich snack.

"I like to go for some type of pasta for carbs, then chicken for protein. I finish my meal with lots of fresh fruit and drink a good amount of water for pre-hydration."

– LB Luke Keuchly, 2013 NFL Defensive Player of the Year

During games, simple carbohydrates are the best option. Examples include oranges, bananas, and energy bars.

> 66 The most important thing when you're starting to run your route is you want to have explosion at the line. You want to create separation from the person that's guarding you. 99

– Nine-time Pro Bowl WR
   Larry Fitzgerald

Arizona Cardinals WR Larry Fitzgerald works out at preseason training camp.

Postgame nutrition is key as well to help kick-start the recovery process. A protein-rich shake is an option that players prefer as it gives them the dense nutrition they need immediately after playing without taking the time that sitting and eating a meal would take. A full meal should still follow one to two hours later, however, consisting of carbs, fruits, and vegetables and more protein.

"Always keep your head up when making a tackle. You have to keep your head up, grab some cloth from the opponent's jersey and drive with your feet until you bring your opponent to the ground."

*– Seven-time Pro Bowl NFL linebacker
   Patrick Willis*

GEAR UP

Players will typically arrive at the stadium three to four hours prior to kickoff, as **ordained** by their personal pregame rituals or by team rules. In the locker room, uniforms and gear will be ready and waiting at the individual players' lockers. At the pro and top college levels, players will go through a few steps before putting that gear on. Players have their own individual routines they like to follow. Some will shower before they get dressed to play. Others will get taped, having trainers wrap problem areas or areas that typically need support based on the position an athlete plays. Players nursing nagging injures will seek treatment for their ailments, which can range from compression wraps to acupuncture and pain injections, anything that allows them to get through the game performing as well as possible. Some players like to relax with a pregame massage. After all of this, it is time to get dressed and head out to the field.

STRETCH

After putting on their gear, players typically take the field for a sequence of stretching. Most teams incorporate a dynamic stretching series that helps to extend range of motion, targeting one muscle group at a time. Stretching before playing football is the best way to prevent

"Losing doesn't make me want to quit, it makes me want to fight that much harder."

– Six-time NCAA national champion coach Paul "Bear" Bryant

Stretching is an essential way of preparing the body to play football and of reducing the risk of injury.

injury. There are a number of methods to perform a dynamic football stretch for various parts of the body. Here are five examples.

Reverse skips (**gluteus maximus**): Skip backward, swinging the arms back in conjunction. Stretching the glute muscle increases sprinting power and reduces the risk of hamstring strains.

Standing knee hugs (hips and gluteus maximus): Alternating legs while standing, raise the knee and wrap your arms around the shin, pulling until the thigh presses against your body. Rise up onto your toes for each hug to activate your calf muscles and work your balance.

> **When you're good at something, you'll tell everyone. When you're great at something, they'll tell you.**
>
> – Two-time NFL MVP RB Walter Payton

Super Bowl champion Walter Payton is the second-leading rusher in NFL history.

Side lunge (gluteus medius): Staying low with feet shoulder-width apart, slowly step far to the right. Keep your toes pointed forward, driving your weight to the right, flexing the knee and hip. Maintain good posture through the entire spine, keeping your head and chest up. Return to the center, and repeat on the left side. This move also stretches the groin and helps prevent injuries there.

Lunge and twist (hip and spine): Stand with feet shoulder-width apart and arms raised to the sides, parallel to the ground. Take a big step forward with the right leg, bringing your weight forward until the knee is over the toes. From this position, twist the torso to the right until the left hand is over the knee. Step back and repeat with the left leg. This stretch helps increase hip mobility for better sprinting power and spine mobility, which reduces stress on the lower back, decreasing the chance of injury.

Inverted hamstring stretches (gluteus maximus and hamstrings): Stand with feet shoulder-width apart and arms raised to the side, parallel to the floor. Lean forward, balancing on the right leg while raising the left leg behind you until it is parallel to the floor. Allow the right knee to flex as the left leg comes up. Hold the position for three to five seconds before slowly lowering the left leg and returning to a standing position. Repeat on the left leg. This is a particularly effective stretch for football players, who suffer a relatively high rate of hamstring injuries.

"I can't stress enough of the importance on lower body strength. It keeps you up for the long haul."

– 2013 NFL sack leader, DE Robert Mathis

WARM-UPS

Once the body has been properly stretched for a solid twenty to thirty minutes, it is ready to be warmed up. These warm-up routines take different shapes across the football world, but most teams will do some light exercise followed by position-specific drills.

Light exercise warm-ups typically consist of movements that focus on agility and coordination, such as progressive sprints, back kicks, the high knee stationary run, and backward and forward jogging.

Players will then split off into groups based on the positions they play. For example, teams might group their players in three: linemen, special teams, and all others. Game plan specific skills are then worked on for each position or group of positions using light or no contact to avoid injury.

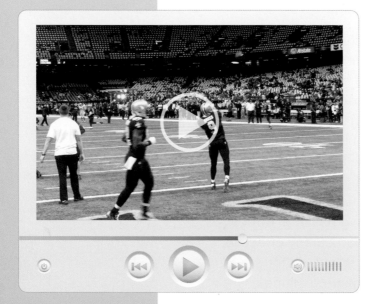

Watch Super Bowl champion QB Drew Brees go through position drills with receivers during pregame warm-ups.

The final phase of the warm-up then follows with the walkthrough. This is an exercise that involves a simulation of plays by both the offense and defense. Both groups should get an equal amount of attention in the walkthrough. The offense-focused plays should be the strongest ones in the playbook, with the defense simulating corresponding coverages that scouting has shown to anticipate from that day's opponent. **Conversely**, the defensive focus should have them defending the particular looks and schemes they expect to see from the opponent.

FOCUS

After the work on the field is finished for the time being, players retreat to the locker room and their own individualized rituals to help them mentally focus on the upcoming task. Some will isolate themselves, lying on the floor with a towel covering their eyes and use the imagery technique to imagine making the plays they need to execute to be successful. Others will use music to clear their minds, headphones on to shut out distractions.

Eliminating distractions is essential to good mental preparation. Success in the sport of football will be elusive without total concentration. Negative thoughts and distractions lay the groundwork for mistakes, which are

"Always watch the hips of the player you're trying to tackle. The head, shoulders and legs can fool and juke you, but the hips never lie."

– NFL linebacker Mychal Kendricks

"When you play corner, there's a lot of twisting and turning, so I make sure to do exercises that include one-leg plant offs, one-leg and one-arm movements and a lot of abs. I also run every day and lift weights at least three days a week."

– Two-time Super Bowl champion CB Ike Taylor

Takeo Spikes played linebacker in the NFL for fifteen seasons.

a sure way to find yourself on the bench. No matter what is going on in players' lives off the field, for the time they are playing, they must concentrate on the game 100 percent. Anything but a total commitment to that day's game is a disservice to yourself and your teammates. Developing a strong football mind and exhibiting the mental toughness that comes with it will help eliminate distractions for the few hours necessary to play a focused game.

"I talk to myself: 'Spikes, you're a better player than that. I know you're better than that. I know you're better than that, so let's prove it.' And I always think, you have one opportunity. Now are you going to tell me, you're going to blow this opportunity? If you walked away from this game, you would be walking away saying 'If I did this or that.' And I don't believe in walking away from something saying "if."

– Takeo Spikes
two-time NFL Pro Bowl linebacker

TEXT-DEPENDENT QUESTIONS:

1. What are three tips to help get a good night's sleep before a game?

2. The pregame meal should be eaten about how many hours before the game?

3. What are some examples of individualized rituals to help football players mentally focus on game day?

RESEARCH PROJECT:

Take some time, and put together a pregame routine for yourself. Be detailed in each element, outlining specific numbers of repetitions for drills, and so on. Be sure to make the routine specific to your position. Outline meals, rest, and all the necessary components that you feel could help best prepare yourself before a big game.

WORDS TO UNDERSTAND:

ambitious: having a desire to be successful, powerful, or famous

imagery: language that causes people to imagine pictures in their minds

intuitive: having the ability to know or understand things without any proof or evidence

Chapter 2

THINK THE GAME

Different coaches will have different approaches to the strategies and tactics of a football game, but the one thing they will certainly agree on universally is that being mentally prepared to play a game is just as important as being physically prepared. Studying the playbook and finding the right mind-set are the equivalent to doing weight training weeks before a season or doing stretches right before a championship. Mental training is as necessary for winning as physical preparation.

SIDEBAR

Sports Meditation

Meditation is used in sports to help athletes center and focus their minds in preparation to play. By meditating before a game, athletes are able to be in a heightened state of mindfulness during their games, and instead of having to analyze the game play by play, they are able to increase the intuitive side of playing football. This means a player is not consciously analyzing what he is doing. Instead of thinking about the game as a series of separate parts, he sees it as a whole, and his mind can make leaps that allow him to act before he is even aware that he has seen an opportunity.

A scientific study in 1974 measured how players did at the same set of tasks, which required coordination, after varying amounts of meditation. The group that meditated the most was best at the coordination tasks.

Using imagery to visualize scoring a touchdown is an effective way to mentally prepare for a game.

Motivating players to do what it takes to be mentally prepared for each game is a big part of a coach's job. Different coaches approach this aspect of game preparation differently. Some use tactics like posting negative comments others have said about the team for all to see in the locker room. Others might insist on a quiet pregame locker room, encouraging players to focus on their upcoming task.

Imagery has proven to help improve player confidence, translating to improved performance. There are other benefits as well. Sports psychologists have discovered that mental imagery is helpful for reducing injuries, while thinking negative thoughts leads to injuries. When players replace self-defeating ideas with more constructive thoughts, they not only make victory more likely, but they also create a safer environment.

One tool to use is positive reinforcement: assure yourself that you will be safe and always in control. Do your best to have fun, and be mindful of changes to your play you wish to make. Doing these mental exercises helps take away a win-at-all-costs attitude that can cause injuries. If you reduce anxiety and control emotions, you will play more confidently—and more safely.

Making time to relax is also important. Before-game relaxation exercises help lower muscular tension. These can also be done even while a game goes on. (This is why we sometimes see players on TV talk to themselves after an important play.) This is called "relaxed attention," staying aware while consciously trying to relax. Injuries are less common when anger and anxiety are controlled by relaxed attention. Decreasing negative emotions also reduces adrenaline, which can cause muscle tension and injury.

When coaches encourage players to get in the zone, it gets players in a mind-set where their minds and bodies are working together calmly, which in turn helps players get the best results on the field.

SEEING SUCCESS: MENTAL IMAGERY

Football coaches will often set goals they want to achieve for their team for each game. This is part of game planning. They may want to have a certain balance of run plays to pass plays or a certain total offense target they are trying to hit. Players should set goals as well as part of their mental preparation. These goals could include rushing for 100 yards or scoring a touchdown. A powerful tool that top players use to help them achieve these goals is imagery. Imagery is the technique of focusing the mind and seeing those goals being accomplished. Running backs see themselves making the cut to cause a defender to miss, bursting through the hole in the defensive line, or jumping high over the goal line to score a touchdown. Defensive ends see themselves making a great spin move to beat the guard and chasing down the quarterback for the sack. They can feel the pads of the quarterback as they wrap him up for the tackle and hear the grunt he makes when they drop him to the ground. Imagery is an effective way for players to mentally get into the game.

The power sweep is one of the oldest tactical plays in football.

Players protect their heads by wearing polycarbonate helmets with face and mouth guards.

It makes sense to set goals that are realistic and can actually be met, but sometimes that may be a matter of perception. In the 1980 Winter Olympic hockey tournament, for example, the U.S. men's team was a heavy underdog to the mighty Soviet Union team in their semifinal game. A realistic goal would have been to score a couple of goals. The Soviets, after all, had Vladislav Tretiak, the best goalie in the world. They had won the last four Olympic gold medals and had lost only once in their last 29 games. Everyone except the American players and coaches expected the United States to lose, but by setting an **ambitious** goal, they were able to come from behind in the final period to steal a 4–3 win in what came to be known as the Miracle on Ice.

RISK CONTROL: SPORTS SUPERSTITIONS

Having a pregame ritual is something fairly common among football players. Many tend to like to do the same things in the same order every time. When players attribute their chances of success to the precise completion of that ritual, however, it becomes a superstition. A quarterback might think that every time he listens to a specific song before a game, his team will win. A lineman may think that if he eats a food related to the rival team's mascot, he will defeat that team. A coach might have a lucky pair of socks he must wear during each game. These are examples of superstitions.

Sports superstitions have compelled psychologists for decades. Psychologist George Gmelch, for example, released an important study on superstition in the 1970s in which he found that when players had an easy task, or they felt in control of what they had to do, they did not think luck was involved, and they felt no need for superstition. Where they developed superstitious behavior was when the tasks became difficult, and players didn't feel they had as much control over outcomes. Gmelch concluded that when athletes are in a situation where chance is involved, and the stakes are high, they are more apt to believe in superstitions.

What are the effects or consequences of superstition? As the psychologist in the study discovered, superstition is our attempt to find control over something that is uncontrollable. We cannot prove whether or not the socks a coach wears makes a difference to the outcome. What was shown, however, is that superstition makes a difference in the confidence level

Studying the playbook as part of being mentally prepared is vital to the success of football players.

of the players who believe in them. If you think you're more in control of elements of chance in a game, then you will play better.

STRATEGIES VERSUS TACTICS

Depending on a superstition is not a good strategy for football coaches or players. Examples of more commonly used strategies, or long-term plans designed to achieve victory or improvement, are relying on a strong defense or taking advantage of speed in the passing game on offense. Strategies usually remain in place for longer periods, such as over an entire football season. Specific actions designed to accomplish a targeted goal are called tactics, and these change from game to game or even within each game.

Common examples of football tactics on offense include the following:

- Off-tackle run: Often led by the fullback, this run aims for the halfback to go through the lane created off of the tackle's block.

- Sweep: One or both of the offensive guards pull from their positions and run parallel to the line of scrimmage before being joined by the fullback to turn upfield and open a lane on one side of the line for the halfback to run through.

- Go route: Also known as a fly route, in this passing play, the wide receiver typically fakes a move to either the inside or outside, or both, before running top speed toward the end zone in hopes of getting behind the pass coverage.

- Post route: The receiver starts straight down the field and then at a predetermined spot breaks toward the goalposts to catch a pass.

Watch five-time NCAA national champion coach Nick Saban break down football tactics.

SIDEBAR

Equipment

With its high-impact collisions, the sport of football subjects its players to a high risk of injury. Especially as more is learned and revealed about the seriousness of head injuries and concussions, it is vitally important that players keep themselves as safe as possible by using the most updated safety equipment. This is especially true of younger players, who are more apt to get hurt because of the increased chance of injury to underdeveloped bones and muscle groups.

To keep their heads in the game, players need to protect their brains. For the head, players wear helmets made of a polycarbonate alloy, which is a very hard plastic that forms the outer shell of the helmet. Experts who say helmets are not safe enough have criticized the use of the material. Polycarbonate helmets were banned in auto racing in 1974 because it was shown to not consistently absorb and redistribute force on crash impact, but rather it would often just crack instead. Auto racing helmets are now made of carbon fiber, which is more expensive to produce. The argument against current football helmets is that while they can be effective in protecting the skull, they do very little to prevent the brain from being jostled and banged against the skull, which is the action that causes concussions. The inside of the helmet contains inflatable air liners along with thick foam pads.

Football helmets also include facemasks, which are made from metal and protect the players from injuries to the face. Players at different positions use different facemasks. Linemen will often use one with more bars, including one that extends up between their eyes to protect the nose better. Skill position players like quarterbacks and receivers use fewer bars to allow the best field of vision. Many players will use a plastic visor set into the facemask to protect their eyes.

Often found attached to the bottom of the facemask is a mouth guard. This molded plastic piece dangles from a strap between plays and is inserted into the mouth and clenched between the teeth to protect them during impact.

The rest of the player's body is protected by a series of pads, most notably for the shoulders, hips, tailbone, knees, and thighs. These pads are made of molded hard plastic affixed over shock-absorbing foam padding.

There are also other types of pads that are specialized by position. Quarterbacks wear flak jacket extensions below their shoulder pads. Linemen use flaps that cover the edges of their pads so their opponents cannot hold onto them. Receivers wear special gloves with rubber palms that grip.

TEXT-DEPENDENT QUESTIONS:

1. What is the technique of focusing the mind and seeing goals being accomplished?

2. What is the difference between a player having a ritual and a superstition?

3. Define tactics.

RESEARCH PROJECT:

Research and outline four commonly used football strategies, two on offense and two on defense. Indicate what factors led to these particular strategies being used. Are they dictated by personnel or by coaching style?

 ## WORDS TO UNDERSTAND:

ligament: a tough piece of tissue in the body that holds bones together or keeps an organ in place

nimble: able to move quickly, easily, and lightly

supple: in regard to the body, able to bend or twist easily

Chapter 3

TRAIN FOR SUCCESS

The other half of the preparation equation that goes along with being mentally ready to play football is getting your body in shape to play. Knowing the playbook backward and forward will only go so far if your body is not properly prepared to execute on every down.

PREGAME PREP

An effective way to help avoid muscle injuries in football is to make sure your muscles are as flexible as possible. When muscles are warm and **supple**, they have the flexibility to better withstand the sudden stopping, starting, and changes of direction that are frequent in football. Cold muscles

Stretching to ensure muscles and ligaments are flexible is an effective way to help avoid injuries.

are more likely to allow for strains or, even worse, muscle pulls or tears. Stretching out muscles and ligaments before you play is preparation time well spent to avoid the lengthy amount of time you might need to recover from an injury.

Warm-up exercises not only stretch the **ligaments** and other connective tissues and raise the temperature inside muscles, but they also prepare the body by making the heart beat faster and the lungs work harder. This brings more oxygen into the body, preparing it aerobically for the endurance a game demands. It is important to use a balanced approach to warm-ups. The idea is to get the body ready to perform optimally, not to burn valuable energy needed to perform well. Think of it like warming up a car engine on

Experts recommend pregame warm-ups include at least fifteen minutes of stretching and calisthenics.

a cold day. Letting the engine run in idle speed for a few minutes gets all its parts lubricated and ready to go, with a full tank of gas waiting to power it when it is time to go.

To recap, a proper warm-up makes your body more flexible, so it can be more **nimble** on the field, which allows for faster response times. Doing a warm-up also helps increase stamina; in other words, you can play harder and feel less tired doing it.

So what is the ideal warm-up time for football players? Experts recommend between ten to fifteen minutes. This window should be extended under cold weather conditions, where muscles will cool down more quickly. In these circumstances, thirty minutes of warm-up should be the goal. Along with stretching, push-ups, sit-ups, jumping jacks, and other calisthenics are also effective in the warm-up process. Players should begin by stretching and warming up the body from the ground up, working the ankles, knees, and hip joints first. It does not make sense to do jumping jacks on legs with cold, tight muscles. If done incorrectly, injuries like the ones they are designed to prevent can occur during warm-ups.

EXERCISES FOR FLEXIBILITY

While stretching is a valuable part of a good warm-up before playing any active sport, the exercises that follow emphasize the parts of the body that are used most in football. While these exercises are beneficial to all football players, each player should stretch the muscles they use most for a game. For example, a quarterback should concentrate on his throwing arm or shoulders; a lineman should stretch his neck and back; wide receivers and defensive backs should work on their legs.

Athletes should always be aware of their own capabilities and limitations. What is helpful and effective for one player may be harmful or cause injury to another. Bodies and body types differ from athlete to athlete, and so should stretching and warm-up regimens. The one listed here is a guide to an effective routine. It should be amended as required to suit each individual player or group of players.

Exercises like pull-ups help build muscle mass football players seek to add in the off-season.

SHOULDERS, CHESTS, AND ARMS

1. Stretch arms upward and backward.
2. Stretch arms straight up; extend arms toward the sky one at a time.
3. Rotate arms forward in circles; move one up as the other descends.
4. Hold each elbow behind the head in a pulling motion.
5. Raise the arms shoulder level, pull them back, and hold the position.

WAIST

Hold arms out to the side, and swing them while you twist the torso back and forth.

BACK, ABDOMEN, AND HIP MUSCLES

While on your back, bend your knees toward your chest, and make a cycling motion with your legs, as if you were riding a bicycle upside down.

Weight training should be reserved for players at the college level or older. Heavy weight training can damage still developing teenage muscles.

LOWER BACK AND THIGHS
Touch your toes while standing or sitting.

HIPS AND HAMSTRINGS
Sit with legs spread and knees locked. Bend forward, and attempt to grasp each ankle. Take turns with each leg; hold the position for around ten seconds.

KNEES AND ANKLES
Lie down, and bring each individual knee toward the chest five times. Take turns with each leg, and hold the position as you slowly rotate your foot.

COOLING DOWN
After a football game, it is helpful to cool down the body following a demanding physical output. Spending just two to five minutes after a hard-fought game to cool down can reduce the chances of conditions such as lightheadedness. Cooldowns slow the heart rate back to normal and return the body to its usual state. Walking, jogging lightly, and stretching again help your body recover after it's been working hard. If you don't have time to jog or stretch, at least don't sit down immediately after a game. If you do, you may find you feel faint. Be sure to walk around until your heart rate is close to normal.

Cooling down after exercising helps slow the heart rate and safely returns the body to its normal state.

OFF-SEASON FITNESS

Gone are the days where players would let themselves get out of shape during the off-season. Today's athletes maintain their conditioning level year-round. Football has one of the shortest seasons, from September to January in most instances, so players need to be especially vigilant with their off-season training. One of the best ways to avoid football injuries is to exercise all year long. Off-season strength and conditioning training is the best insurance against the rigors of the game that come when football is back in season. Off-season fitness can be maintained by general aerobic exercise like running, swimming, or cycling. Playing other sports during the off-season like soccer, tennis, basketball, or racquetball can also be good aerobic exercise to keep the heart and lungs in top shape.

Check out these highlights of the off-season workout program at the University of Texas.

Closer to the season, a football player should work on conditioning exercises that emphasize strength, speed, and endurance. He should pay attention to muscle groups that are used most in games. Exercises like pull-ups and sprinting will build and tone muscle mass as well as increase endurance.

TRAINING: HOW MUCH AND HOW OFTEN?

Training too much, without giving your body time to recover, can also cause injuries. Any good training plan should have built-in days off and should not have too many days in row of the same kind of training. Although training guidelines and requirements can be found for every level of football from Pop Warner to the NFL, proper training should never be about putting in a certain number of hours in a given time frame. The emphasis on training should be on the quality and consistency of training rather than its quantity.

Players need to be careful to avoid overtraining. If the body is showing signs of stress, like muscle soreness or stiffness, or if players feel constant fatigue, they may be overtraining. Overtraining usually results in poor performance on the football field. Symptoms of overtraining are usually temporary and can be reversed with rest, but it is better to avoid them altogether as the recovery time may cause players to miss playing time. Training too much, without giving your body time to recover, can also cause injuries. This is especially true of repetitive stress injuries that may result from lifting weights too many days in row. While overdoing it may be tempting during intense periods of training, both in the off-season and in between games, smart players will space out difficult training days with days of rest.

For teenagers, any type of intense weight training is too much. For still developing teenage bodies, heavy weight training is not a good idea. While the body is growing, it is likely to be damaged by this form of training.

TEXT-DEPENDENT QUESTIONS:

1. What kinds of muscles are more likely to allow for strains or, even worse, muscle pulls or tears?

2. Name three areas of the body most important to stretch before playing football.

3. What are some signs from the body that it is being overtrained?

 ## RESEARCH PROJECT:

Look into what is required to put together an effective off-season training program. What types of non-football activities are best to keep players in football shape? How might off-season training vary by position?

WORDS TO UNDERSTAND:

chronic: continuing or occurring again for a long time

grappling: struggling hand to hand

notorious: well-known or famous, especially for something bad

vertebrae: the small bones that are linked together to form the backbone

Chapter 4

TAKING CARE OF THE BODY: INJURIES AND NUTRITION

According to a 2013 report by the nonprofit advocacy group Safe Kids Worldwide, nearly 400,000 children age six to nineteen go to the emergency room each year with football-related injuries. The College Football Assistance Fund reports more than 20,000 injuries in college football each year. And in the NFL, about 400 players suffer injury every season. While the NFL has the highest percentage rate of injury, adolescent players are especially vulnerable to injury because their bodies are still growing. In grade school, injuries are less common because the game is played at low speed and is low impact as the players do not weigh very much. In high school, however, players are larger, stronger, and faster— which means when collisions occur, they are significantly more violent and more likely to cause injury. When high school players do get hurt, the injury is also apt to be more serious.

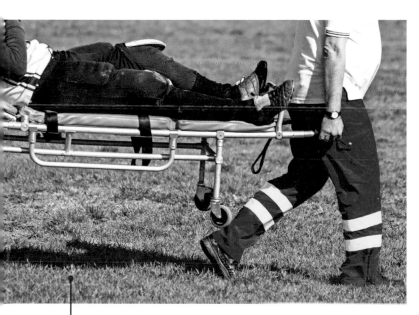

Nearly 400,000 kids age six to nineteen go to emergency rooms around the country each year with football-related injuries.

There are two types of football injuries: acute injuries and repetitive stress injuries.

An acute injury is a sudden injury typically caused by a trauma. In football, an example would be a broken bone caused by a collision with another player or a torn ligament or tendon caused by torque from a sudden change of direction.

A repetitive stress injury, on the other hand, is one caused by overuse of a muscle or tendon that results in a condition of constant pain. Overuse injuries are specific to different types of football players. A quarterback may have **chronic** pain in his elbow or shoulder, while a defensive lineman might overwork his lower back muscles. The dull ache of overuse injury may seem less important than an acute injury (such as a broken bone), but these injuries also require medical attention. In football, certain parts of the body are more likely to be injured than others.

Acute injuries are those that occur during a specific moment on the field, like broken bones or torn ligaments.

FOOT AND ANKLE

In football, feet take large amounts of physical stress at all positions. Therefore foot and ankle injuries are common to all players. In the close-quarters combat along the line of scrimmage, it is not unusual for linemen to step on each other's feet. In the secondary, both defensive backs and wide receivers do a lot of jumping and landing on their feet, which can lead to ankle sprains and fractures in the small bones of the foot.

The Most Common Football Injuries

- Contusions (bruises) caused by a direct hit: These are most common in the thighs. Contusions result in direct swelling—and possibly bleeding—in muscles or other tissues. A deep thigh bruise can impair muscle function and cause players to miss playing time.

- Ankle sprains and strains: Ankles are susceptible to soft tissue damage (ligaments and tendons) when pivoting, changing direction, or putting too much pressure on the joint.

- ACL tear: The anterior cruciate ligament (ACL) of the knee is susceptible to damage in collisions from the front or rear.

- MCL tear: The medial collateral ligament (MCL) of the knee is susceptible to damage in collisions from the side.

- Meniscus tear: When a player rotates his body while a foot stays planted, the knee can twist, causing the meniscus (a section of knee cartilage) to tear.

- Pulled hamstring: Bursts of speed can cause the hamstrings (the three muscles that run the length of the back of each upper leg) to pull or even tear.

- Tendinitis: This repetitive stress injury (resulting in tendon inflammation in the joint) is especially common in the throwing shoulder or elbow of quarterbacks.

- Shoulder separation: A direct blow to the shoulder can cause a separation of the acromioclavicular joint, meaning the ligaments that attach the collarbone to the shoulder blade are torn.

- Fractured clavicle: A common bone to break in football, this injury usually occurs upon impact with the ground.

- Concussion: This is a mild traumatic brain injury caused by a blow to the head, which can have long-term consequences if not treated immediately and cautiously.

Fractures can be acute injuries, but they can also be caused by overuse. Football players often have stress fractures: tiny cracks in the bone's surface caused by constant physical stress. Receivers are especially vulnerable to stress fractures in their feet and ankles because they frequently jump up for passes and then land hard, often awkwardly if they are battling for the ball with an opponent. The chronic pain of a stress fracture can eventually lead to a limp. A doctor should be consulted even if the pain seems not very serious. The most likely therapy to be employed is the R.I.C.E. (Rest, Ice, Compression, Elevation) program, with an emphasis on the R (rest).

Quick changes of direction can overstress ligaments, pushing them out of their normal angles and making sprained ankles another common football injury. Sprains are **notorious** for recurring, so the injury should be carefully monitored throughout the season. The closer a player follows his doctor's rehabilitation exercises, the lower chance there is of an injury happening in the same place again.

KNEES AND LEGS

There are multitudes of ways that legs and knees get injured in football. Being tackled below the knees can cause knee and leg injuries. Quick turns or being twisted in the upper body while the foot is planted is also a common way most of these injuries are inflicted. The most common injuries

The knee is very prone to injury in football, and ACL tears are a common form of football knee injury.

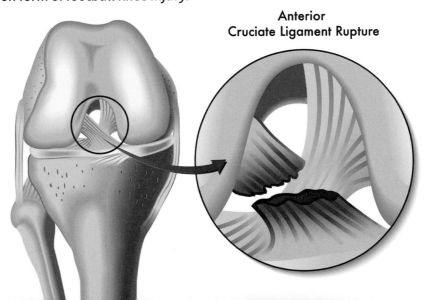

Anterior
Cruciate Ligament Rupture

for the knee and leg are sprains, strains, fractures, and dislocations. They range in seriousness from a twisted knee to a broken leg. Some of the most common include the following:

- Knee sprains: A ligament in the joint is stretched. R.I.C.E. is the best therapy.

- Hamstring pulls: The muscles at the back of the thigh are strained. R.I.C.E is again employed.

- A dislocated kneecap (also called a patella): A hard tackle can knock the kneecap off to one side, and surgery is typically required to put the kneecap back into its proper position.

- Contusions and bruises: Players often cause contusions by hitting their helmets against another player's thigh. Compression and ice are used to treat these injuries.

- Leg fractures: These are extremely painful and can end a player's season. Crutches need to be used, and X-rays are usually required for a medical diagnosis. The bone is set, with surgery sometimes required.

HIP, RIB, AND BACK INJURIES

Quarterbacks are the players most likely to suffer bruised or broken ribs, typically from being hit broadside while throwing a pass. Linemen commonly suffer back injuries, which are typically repetitive stress strains and spasms.

- Hip pointer injuries: These are bruises at the upper ridge of the pelvis.

- Strained adductor muscles (which are located under the hips): This can be caused by being forced sideways on the field.

- Rib injuries: These are painful, and X-rays are needed to determine if the rib is broken or just bruised Even if the fractured rib is not separated, it takes about six weeks of rest to heal. A flack jacket can be used, so a player is able to avoid missing playing time.

- Sprained back: Players often use braces to recover from this.

- "Slipped" disk: A severe blow to the back may cause the disk between two vertebrae to bulge out of place, putting pressure on nerves and causing acute pain. Treatment includes medication, wearing a neck collar, traction, and sometimes surgery.

- **Vertebrae** fractures: These can occur if the back is bent backward by a forceful impact or as a result of a direct impact to the spine. A fracture is rare but dangerous. Recovery should take at least six weeks, and players with a minor fracture may need to wear a neck brace until the bone heals, which may take up to six to eight weeks. In some cases, surgery is required.

SHOULDERS, ARMS, AND WRISTS

Falling to or being driven into the ground while being tackled causes many shoulder, arm, and wrist injuries. Finger injuries are very common among linemen, who use their hands in **grappling** battles on every play. Defensive players that make tackles many times in a game are especially prone to shoulder, arm, and wrist injuries:

- A separated shoulder: This results when a ligament tears at the end of the collarbone (or clavicle). The clavicle can be raised up slightly. The best treatment is rest and then strengthening exercises.

- A dislocated shoulder: This is a more serious injury than a bone separation. It involves the shoulder popping out of the socket because of a loose ligament or torn cartilage. X-rays are needed to diagnose this. The injured players usually wear a shoulder sling for about three weeks. Only the most serious dislocations require surgery.

- Broken bones: These are often treated temporarily on the sideline with a splint. (Some players have finished games believing they were only suffering from a sprain.) X-rays are needed to diagnose broken bones, which will then be immobilized in a cast. Bone usually requires at least six weeks to heal.

NECKS AND HEADS

Head and neck injuries are the most dangerous kind in football, and leagues at all levels have implemented rules about how and when to tackle players

Concussions are potentially serious head injuries, and most leagues have steps in place to identify when players may have suffered a concussion.

to reduce these types of injuries specifically. Neck injuries usually happen while the heads of players are lowered. Head injuries are typically caused by direct contact from another player's helmet, knee, or the ground. Neck injuries vary in severity, while head injuries are usually more serious. These injuries include the following:

- Stingers: When the nerves of the neck stretch too far, it causes a stinging pain and temporary numbness that is referred to as a stinger. While these symptoms are temporary, players should make coaches or trainers aware of them.

- Whiplash: This occurs when a player's neck snaps backward, causing a sprain or strain in the neck. Doctors use neck collars or braces to aid recovery.

- Neck fractures: These involve the spinal cord and are very serious. A player with a neck fracture should not be moved since doing so could cause paralysis or even death. That's why players on the ground need to stay where they are until emergency help arrives and the seriousness of the injury is determined. These players may have their heads immobilized on the field and be carried off on a backboard as a precaution.

- Concussions: A concussion is an injury to the brain caused by a blow that sometimes causes a lack of consciousness. More than 90 percent of concussions are mild, but all concussions can cause problems like headaches, lack of alertness, fainting, difficulty sleeping, light sensitivity, and loss of short-term memory. Most leagues have protocols

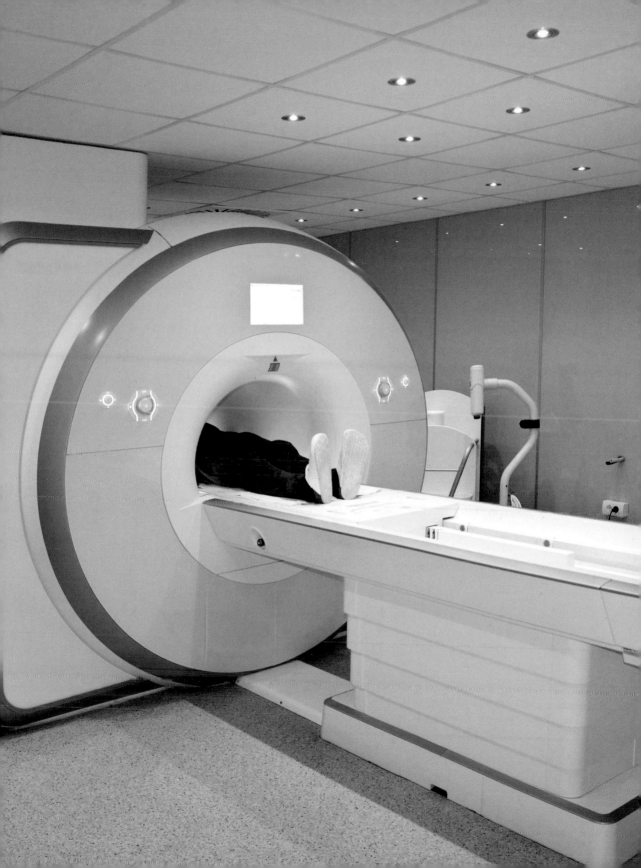

in place to immediately assess any player that has received a blow to the head before allowing him to rejoin the game. Because concussions vary widely in their symptoms, imaging tests are needed. A player should not play for up to four weeks after the symptoms disappear.

- Hematoma: A blow to the head could cause a fatal hematoma, which involves bleeding under the skull. If bleeding continues, pressure on the brain increases as well. Less severe hematomas clear up by themselves, but surgery may be required to remove blood clots. Players and coaches should assume that all head injuries are serious.

NUTRITION

A key component of the physical preparation that can help to reduce the chance of injury is nutrition. Eating well is crucial to an athlete's overall wellness. Players at the NFL level are obviously skilled at playing football, but the best players, along with exercising and training hard, have regulated their diets for years. Achieving remarkable amounts of muscle mass requires intense amounts of discipline. However, the benefits of maintaining healthy nutrition are greater than just being able to play the game at a higher level; a healthy diet will also lead to fewer injuries on the field. Knowing what to eat, when to eat it, and how often to eat is important. There are decisions to be made: What kind of diet is right for your body? Should dietary supplements be a part of your nutrition regimen?

Football players in training should consume about 4,000 calories per day, 60 percent of which should come from carbohydrates like pasta.

Fruits and leafy vegetables are the best options for a variety of vitamins and minerals from their original source.

HOW MUCH TO EAT

The Unites States Department of Agriculture (USDA) states that the typical adult man age twenty-one to thirty-five should eat between 2,400 and 3,000 calories per day depending on how active he is. For an athlete like a football player, however, that amount will not begin to provide the fuel needed for success. Players need to build and maintain larger amounts of muscle mass and therefore should consume more than 4,000 calories every day. In some very intense preseason sessions, players who are at the top of their game have been known to consume up to 10,000 calories, five times more than an inactive person. Remember, though, to always consult your doctor or dietician before making any dramatic changes to your diet. Many sports dieticians recommend that football players not consume all their calories in three large meals each day but instead eat smaller amounts of food more often. This approach gives your body a steady amount of energy during training.

WHEN TO EAT

Timing is important with eating and drinking water. A football player should eat a small meal between a half-hour to an hour before he trains. Also, athletes should drink large amounts of water (twenty ounces) one to two hours before a practice. While exercising, players should continue drinking to stay hydrated but with smaller amounts of water. Immediately after exercising, a small snack is a good idea, and around an hour after training, a player should have a larger meal.

Learn about the importance of good nutrition to a major college football program.

WHAT TO EAT

Players should be getting a majority of their calories from carbohydrates (about 60 percent). This is known as carbo-loading. These foods supply the body with energy. Sweet potatoes, oats, wild rice, bananas, and chickpeas are examples of good carbohydrates. Fruit, plain yogurt, and whole wheat pasta are also good sources of fuel. It is important to stress that these are good carbohydrates, ones that contain natural sugars and starches. Athletes should avoid carbohydrates that contain lots of white sugar, including sugary energy drinks; water is the best drink option. Refined sugar contains zero nutrients, and the liver can only metabolize it in small amounts. Any excess amounts that the liver cannot process are turned into fat and stored in the body.

After a workout, a football player should eat foods like lean meats (chicken or tuna) that are high in

Fish, nuts, and milk are among the healthy options to include protein in the diet, which is a key ingredient to building the muscle football players need.

protein. These foods will help the body repair damaged muscles. Another tip concerns hydration. Before and after you work out, weigh yourself. If your body lost weight, drink a cup of water for every pound that you lost.

DIETARY SUPPLEMENTS

An athlete who maintains a healthy, balanced diet should not take additional supplements. Nutritious, natural food is the best way to get the nutrients your body needs. You should only take supplements if for some reason you cannot get enough of something your body needs through the food you eat.

VITAMIN AND MINERAL TABLETS

The right diet choices will provide football players with the vitamins they need to perform at their best on the field. Foods like fruit, green leafy vegetables, fish, nuts, and milk contain vitamins and minerals from their original sources and are the best options. Sometimes this is not possible when hasty food decisions need to be made, like eating at a restaurant where much of the food may be processed or fried, stripping it of nutrients. Not all players have access to the best food all the time, so a vitamin and mineral supplement could be integrated into a healthy diet in these cases.

There are specific pills for a single vitamin or mineral that a diet is lacking. Multivitamins are supplements that contain a mixture of vitamins and nutrients.

Supplement use should be handled carefully. A mineral or vitamin can be helpful in small amounts but become dangerous in large proportions. You can overdose on vitamins, which can result in a multitude of side effects that can be strange or even scary (loss of vision, numbness, or liver damage). Talk to your doctor before taking any supplement.

PROTEIN SUPPLEMENTS

Just as with vitamins and minerals, food is the body's best source of protein (the nutrient found in meat and dairy products). Protein helps your muscles repair themselves—but immediately after a workout, you probably won't feel

Protein shakes can help provide efficient protein boosts when needed, such as immediately following games or workouts.

like eating a large, nutritious meal, and you may not have time immediately after winning a big game when your body needs it most. Protein shakes can offer a quick fix in these situations. These products usually contain proteins with low amounts of carbohydrates and fats; some include vitamins as well. Drinking protein shakes after your workouts and games can help keep your muscles healthy.

A nutritionist can help you fit protein shakes into your diet in the most effective way possible. Remember that protein shakes, if needed, can supplement a lack of protein intake. However, any shake cannot replace a balanced diet, no matter how many nutrients are in it.

TEXT-DEPENDENT QUESTIONS:

1. What is a repetitive stress injury?

2. Because a football player needs to build and maintain larger amounts of muscle mass, how many calories should he consume every day?

3. When should an athlete take additional dietary supplements?

RESEARCH PROJECT:

Put together three different nutrition plans for players at three different positions: offensive lineman, linebacker, and wide receiver. Be sure to account for the different goals players in these positions have in terms of weight, energy expenditure, and so on.

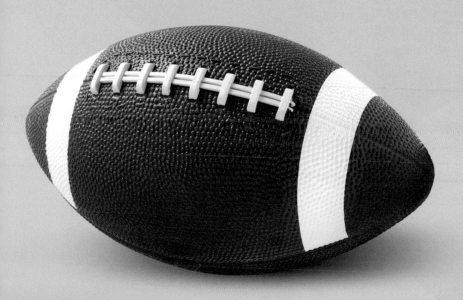

 WORDS TO UNDERSTAND:

exhibition: the act of showing something in public

exploits: exciting acts or actions

marquee: very popular and well-known

FOOTBALL: FROM SAMMY BAUGH TO SUPER BOWLS AND SUNDAYS ABROAD

WALTER CAMP TO THE NFL

In 1880, Walter Camp was the captain of the football team at Yale University in Connecticut, but he was not happy about it. The sport was in its infancy, and Camp felt the rules, or lack of them, made the sport disorderly and dull. At the annual rules convention for the sport that year, he proposed a number of rule changes that forever changed the game.

The line of scrimmage was one of the many elements of the modern game introduced by Walter Camp, one of the pioneers of American football.

The most significant of these changes was the introduction of the line of scrimmage. Camp also came up with the snap back to the quarterback. He would continue to come up with rule changes for the next four decades. In 1881 he established a standard field size. In 1882, his last year as a player, Camp came up with the down and distance rules so that teams could not control the ball for the entire game. He implemented a new scoring system in 1883 that made the touchdown a scoring play (they were worth four points; field goals were worth five). Camp also introduced tackling below the waist and the concept of blocking.

Camp's influence distinctly shaped and established the sport of football as its own game, but he resisted a number of future innovations that exist in its modern version. Camp was opposed to the huddle and the three-point stance for linemen, who were required to stand up straight. Forward passing was permitted, but throws were limited to certain distances to be legal, and if a pass fell incomplete, it was a turnover.

In 1921, league president Joe Carr changed the name from the American Professional Football Association to the National Football League (NFL).

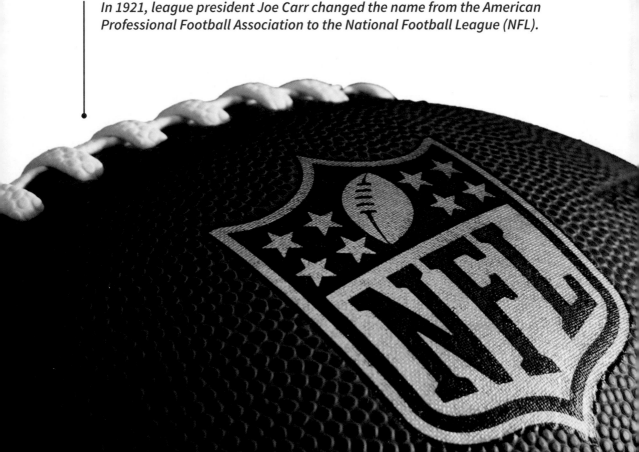

The Arizona Cardinals and Chicago Bears are the only two founding franchises of the NFL remaining today. The Cardinals started out in Chicago before moving to St. Louis in 1959 and Arizona in 1988. The Bears started in nearby Decatur, Illinois, before moving to Chicago in 1921.

In the late nineteenth century, football continued to evolve and thrive at the college level, especially in the East. By the turn of the century, local club teams paid the best players, who offered their services to the highest bidder as there were no contracts and little team loyalty existed. These were the first professional football players.

The most famous of the early professionals was Olympic hero Jim Thorpe. A two-time Olympic gold medalist at the 1912 Games in Sweden, Thorpe was also a two-time All-American running back in college and one of the most famous athletes in the country. When he signed to play for the Canton Bulldogs in 1915, it was a big deal. Five years later, Thorpe would become the president of the American Professional Football Association (APFA), the first professional football league. Thorpe stepped down after one year, replaced by Joe Carr, a sportswriter from Columbus, Ohio, who ran one of the league's teams, the Columbus Panhandles. It is Carr who changed the league name to the National Football League in 1921. Carr's eighteen-year term as president was very influential. He drafted the first league constitution. Carr was committed to bringing NFL football to big cities. Some of the league's most famous franchises joined the NFL during Carr's watch, including the New York Giants, Chicago Bears, and Pittsburgh Steelers. In 1925, he introduced the first standard player contracts. That year saw the formation of a rival to Carr's league.

The agent of Notre Dame football star Red Grange, a man named C. C. Pyle, started the American Football League (AFL). Pyle had arranged an **exhibition** tour for the Bears featuring his star client after Grange graduated in 1925. After the wildly successful tour, however, Pyle advised his client not to sign the standard player contract with the Bears and elected instead to form his own league. The AFL began with nine teams, competing head to head with the NFL in New York, Brooklyn, Chicago, and Philadelphia and battled to sign players and grab headlines.

The first season of play in the AFL was 1926, and scheduling was very erratic, with some teams playing as many as fifteen games and others as few as four. Outside of New York, where Grange attracted crowds, and Philadelphia, the new league struggled. The NFL had more than twenty teams that season, although it had expanded too quickly. Franchises folded in both leagues, and by the end of the year, the AFL shut down. The NFL was down to just eleven teams and absorbed Grange's New York Yankees, the only survivor of the AFL.

Part of the reason for the struggles of the sport was the sport itself. Despite electrifying athletes like Thorpe and Grange, football was dull. The game was low scoring, and shutouts were common as the rules hampered offense and lent themselves to defensive strategies. Passing was a little-employed component for coaches at the time.

Chicago owner George Halas wanted to change that, but for years he lacked a catalyst to demonstrate how entertaining the game could be if the offense was opened up. Then Slingin' Sammy Baugh came along.

QUARTERBACKS AND SUPER BOWLS

Baugh was the quarterback at Texas Christian University (TCU) in 1936, his senior year. That season he threw for more than 1,000 yards for the second straight year, which was almost unheard of. Up to 80,000 fans were turning up at TCU home games to watch Baugh throw. Washington owner George Preston Marshall heard the stories of Baugh's **exploits** during a business trip to Texas, and when he investigated, Marshall knew he had to have Baugh in Washington. He drafted Baugh sixth overall in 1937, and the college quarterback sensation was an instant professional star. With Baugh at the helm, the forward pass was a first choice rather than a last resort for the Washington offense, and the team went on to win the NFL championship in Baugh's rookie season.

Baugh gave Halas the ammunition he needed to convince the other owners to change the sport. He spearheaded efforts to change restrictive rules, making passing a vital part of the sport and changing football forever. Baugh was the brightest of a legion of stars that helped grow the league's popularity in the 1930s and 1940s, along with Green Bay receiver Don Hutson, Bears RB Bronko Nagurski, and his teammate, QB Sid Luckman.

In Chicago, Luckman was Halas's Baugh, winning four championships for his visionary owner from 1939 to 1950. The aerial attack style that led Luckman and Baugh to a combined five championships in seven seasons from 1937 to 1946 was adopted almost league wide, laying the groundwork for the rise of the passing game that dominates football today.

The Cleveland Browns were named in 1946 for their original coach, Paul Brown, who pioneered the use of playbooks and IQ tests for players and led the way in integrating the league.

In 1946, legendary coach Paul Brown had a momentous year. He took a job coaching a team in Cleveland in the newly formed league called the All-America Football Conference (AAFC). The coach who innovated the use of playbooks, IQ tests for players, and forty-yard dash timing, among others, made history when he voluntarily signed two black players (future Hall of Famers Marion Motley and Bill Willis), a move that led to the racial integration of professional football. Brown also signed QB Otto Graham out of Northwestern that year, a move that helped his team, called the Browns, win all four of the AAFC championships before the league folded. The Browns joined the NFL in 1950, and Brown and Graham won three more championships in the NFL.

Thanks to stars like Graham, the NFL was a popular sport in the 1950s, but college football was the version of the game fans cared most about.

That changed, however, on December 28, 1958. This is the date that the 1958 NFL championship game between the Baltimore Colts and the New York Giants was played. The game was broadcast across the country on television, a rarity in those days for NFL games. At halftime, however, the game was failing to take advantage of its exposure on the national stage. Baltimore led just 14–3. In the third quarter, however, the Giants came to life and took a 17–14 lead. The crowd in the stadium and those watching at home were riveted. Baltimore kicked a field goal with just seven seconds left to force overtime. The Colt's star QB, Johnny Unitas, led an overtime drive that covered seventy-nine yards in twelve plays, down to the New York one-yard line. The Colts were on the verge of winning, and the drama was high. It went even higher when the TV signal was lost

seconds before the play from the one-yard line. NBC sent an employee out onto the field pretending to be drunk, so they could stall until they fixed the problem. The picture came back on just in time to see the Colts run in the winning touchdown.

When Jets' QB Joe Namath made good on his guarantee to beat the NFL's Colts in Super Bowl III, the win legitimized the AFL and forced a merger between the leagues.

The game, which was instantly labeled "The Greatest Game Ever Played," was the talk of the country, and all of a sudden, Unitas was America's biggest sports hero, and pro football was all the rage. Texas oil millionaire Lamar Hunt decided that the NFL was something he had to be a part of. The league, however, did not feel the same way about him, blocking his attempt to start an NFL franchise in Dallas. So Hunt started his own league, reviving the old American Football League name from the 1920s. The AFL began play in 1960 in eight cities, competing with the NFL for players throughout

Led by QB Terry Bradshaw and a punishing defense, the Pittsburgh Steelers won four Super Bowls in six seasons in the 1970s.

the decade. In 1967, the NFL agreed to a championship game between the two league champions. The first interleague championship game was played between the NFL's Green Bay Packers and AFL champs the Kansas City Chiefs. Green Bay won easily, and in 1968, the Packers again won, this time over Oakland. It was in 1969 that the championship officially became known as the Super Bowl, and the game now known as Super Bowl III changed football again.

NAMATH, MONTANA, BRADY, AND BEYOND

Super Bowl III featured the NFL champion Baltimore Colts against the AFL upstarts from New York, the Jets. Their flamboyant and outspoken quarterback, Joe Namath, led the Jets. Namath famously guaranteed a win for the Jets, despite being a huge underdog to their NFL opponents. Namath backed up his prediction by leading the Jets to a 16–7 upset over the Colts, a win that instantly legitimized the AFL. Before the next football season began, the two leagues agreed to a merger, creating the two-conference model (with the AFC and the NFC) that makes up the NFL today.

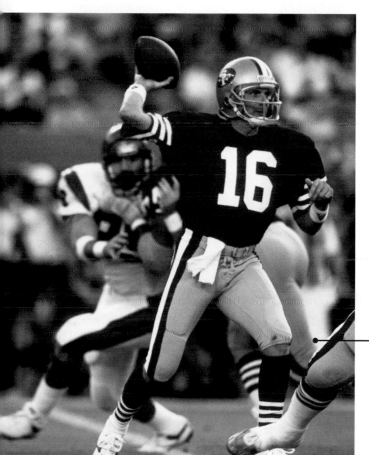

The new look league thrived in the 1970s behind the success of **marquee** franchises like the Pittsburgh Steelers (who won four Super Bowls in the decade), Miami Dolphins, and Dallas Cowboys. In 1979, the San Francisco 49ers drafted a quarterback out of Notre Dame in the third round. Three other quarterbacks

San Francisco QB Joe Montana led his team to a Super Bowl win in his first season as the starter and went on to win three more Super Bowls in his Hall of Fame career.

were drafted ahead of him, but Joe Montana would go on to prove that the decision not to pick him was a mistake.

Montana spent his rookie season primarily as the backup quarterback on the 49er roster. When he took over as starter in 1981, he led the team to a 13–3 record and its first Super Bowl win. Montana led the 49ers to three more Super Bowl victories in the 1980s. Montana ended his Hall of Fame career with his retirement in 1995.

Five years later, another quarterback who was passed over in the entry draft even more than Montana entered the NFL. The New England

New England QB Tom Brady has won five Super Bowls, despite being a sixth-round draft pick.

Patriots selected Michigan's Tom Brady in the sixth round of the 2000 draft, the 199th player and seventh quarterback taken. Brady has had one of the most spectacular careers in NFL history, winning five Super Bowls and four MVPs through the 2016 season.

Brady is still one of the best quarterbacks in the game, despite the fact that he turned forty in 2017. He cannot play forever, however, so which quarterback will be the future face of an NFL that has fully embraced the passing game as the preferred method of generating offense and fan interest? Indianapolis QB Andrew Luck is a good bet to inherit the role.

Luck turns just twenty-eight in 2017, and the first overall pick from the 2012 draft has all the talent needed to dominate the quarterback position for the next decade. His main rivals are the number-one pick from the year previous to Luck, Cam Newton of Carolina, and Russell Wilson, drafted in the third round by Seattle the same year as Luck. Both Wilson and Newton have led their teams to Super Bowls, and Wilson's team actually won the Super Bowl to cap the 2013 season, while Newton was the 2015 MVP. But Luck's talent is undeniable, leading his team to the playoffs in each of his first three seasons, including to the 2014 AFC championship game, where he lost to Brady and the Patriots.

Check out these Andrew Luck highlights.

One of the most intriguing questions facing the NFL in the future involves where stars like Luck will be showcasing their skills. In 2016, Luck and the Colts played their fourth game of the season against Jacksonville at Wembley Stadium in London, England. This was the tenth consecutive season London has hosted a regular season NFL game as part of the NFL International Series. In 2014 and 2015, London hosted three games per season. In 2016 London again hosted three games, while a fourth international regular season game was held in Mexico City. The first regular season game played in Mexico happened back in 2005. The Buffalo Bills also played a regular season game in Toronto, Canada, each season from 2008 to 2013.

The NFL has made no secret of the fact that the league would like to have an international franchise, and London has the population, fan base, and stadium facilities to support an NFL franchise. There are a number of hurdles to clear to make this wish a reality, however. These include logistical considerations like travel back and forth from London, especially during playoff time and how that would affect scheduling. A determination would also need to be made on whether a London-based team would come about through expansion or relocation.

In October of 2015, NFL International Executive Vice President Mark Waller told the press at a meeting in London before that season's game, "We have always said that we felt that we started in 2007 with the games, and we felt it was a 15-year process so that would give us years '21, '22 and that feels sort of right—five or six years." International expansion appears to be a matter of when rather than if for the future of the NFL.

The NFL has played regular season games in London, England, since 2007.

TEXT-DEPENDENT QUESTIONS:

1. What was Walter Camp's role in football?

2. What happened in "The Greatest Game Ever Played"?

3. What are some of the cities outside the United States that have hosted NFL games in recent years, signaling a possibility for the NFL to have an international franchise?

RESEARCH PROJECT:

If the NFL were to expand internationally, which city would be the best location? Do a comparison outlining three pros and three cons for each of London, Toronto, and Mexico City.

SERIES GLOSSARY OF KEY TERMS

Acute Injury: Usually the result of a specific impact or traumatic event that occurs in one specific area of the body, such as a muscle, bone, or joint.

Calories: units of heat used to indicate the amount of energy that foods will produce in the human body.

Carbohydrates: substances found in certain foods (such as bread, rice, and potatoes) that provide the body with heat and energy and are made of carbon, hydrogen, and oxygen.

Cardiovascular: of or relating to the heart and blood vessels.

Concussion: a stunning, damaging, or shattering effect from a hard blow—especially a jarring injury of the brain resulting in a disturbance of cerebral function.

Confidence: faith in oneself and one's abilities without any suggestion of conceit or arrogance.

Cooldown: easy exercise, done after more intense activity, to allow the body to gradually transition to a resting or near-resting state.

Dietary Supplements: products taken orally that contain one or more ingredient (such as vitamins or amino acids) that are intended to supplement one's diet and are not considered food.

Dynamic: having active strength of body or mind.

Electrolytes: substances (such as sodium or calcium) that are ions in the body regulating the flow of nutrients into and waste products out of cells.

Flexible: applies to something that can be readily bent, twisted, or folded without any sign of injury.

Hamstrings: any of three muscles at the back of the thigh that function to flex and rotate the leg and extend the thigh.

Hydration: to supply with ample fluid or moisture.

Imagery: mental images, the products of imagination.

Mind-Set: a mental attitude or inclination.

Overuse Injury: an injury that is most likely to occur to the ankles, knees, hands, and wrists, due to the excessive use of these body parts during exercise and athletics.

Plyometrics: also known as "jump training" or "plyos," exercises in which muscles exert maximum force in short intervals of time, with the goal of increasing power (speed and strength).

Positive Mental Attitude (PMA): the philosophy that having an optimistic disposition in every situation in one's life attracts positive changes and increases achievement.

Protein: a nutrient found in food (as in meat, milk, eggs, and beans) that is made up of many amino acids joined together, is a necessary part of the diet, and is essential for normal cell structure and function.

Quadriceps: the greater extensor muscle of the front of the thigh that is divided into four parts.

Recovery: the act or process of becoming healthy after an illness or injury.

Resistance: relating to exercise, involving pushing against a source of resistance (such as a weight) to increase strength. Strength training, or resistance exercises, are those that build muscle. They create stronger and larger muscles by producing more and tougher muscle fibers to cope with the increasing weight demands.

Strategy: a careful plan or method.

Stretching: to extend one's body or limbs from a cramped, stooping, or relaxed position.

Tactics: actions or methods that are planned and used to achieve a particular goal.

Tendon: a tough piece of tissue in the body that connects a muscle to a bone.

Training: the process by which an athlete prepares for competition by exercising, practicing, and so on.

Warm-Up: exercise or practice especially before a game or contest—broadly, to get ready.

Workout: a practice or exercise to test or improve one's fitness for athletic competition, ability, or performance.

FURTHER READING:

Luke, Andrew. *Football (Inside the World of Sports)*. Broomall, PA: Mason Crest, 2017.

Editors of Sports Illustrated. *Sports Illustrated NFL Quarterback (QB): The Greatest Position in Sports*. New York: Sports Illustrated, 2014

Puldutor, Seth. *Drew Brees (Superstars of Pro Football)*. Broomall, PA: Mason Crest, 2013

Biskup, Agnieszka. *Football (The Science of Sports [Sports Illustrated for Kids])*. North Mankato, MN: Capstone Press, 2014

INTERNET RESOURCES:

FDA: Dietary Supplements: *http://www.fda.gov/Food/DietarySupplements/default.htm*

NFL: *http://www.nfl.com*

Sports Training Advisor: *www.sport-fitness-advisor.com/football-training.html*

Pro Football Reference: *http://www.pro-football-reference.com*

VIDEO CREDITS:

Watch Super Bowl champion QB Drew Brees go through position drills with receivers during pregame warm-ups: *http://x-qr.net/1Gt1*

Watch five-time NCAA national champion coach Nick Saban break down football tactics: *http://x-qr.net/1HBN*

Check out these highlights of the off-season workout program at the University of Texas: *http://x-qr.net/1HM*P

Learn about the importance of good nutrition to a major college football program: *http://x-qr.net/1HhJ*

Check out these Andrew Luck highlights: *http://x-qr.net/1GyH*

PICTURE CREDITS

QR CODES AND LINKS TO THIRD-PARTY CONTENT

INDEX

In this index, page numbers in ***bold italics*** font indicate photos or videos.

ABOUT THE AUTHOR

Peter Douglas is a former journalist, reporting on both sports and general news for many years at television stations in various locations across the US affiliated with NBC, CBS and Fox. Prior to his journalism career he worked with the Boston Red Sox Major League baseball team. An avid writer and sports enthusiast, he has authored 16 additional books on sports topics. In his downtime Peter enjoys family time with his wife and two young children and attending hockey and baseball games in his home city.